大师经典文库

Sun Tzu

孙 子 兵 法
The Art of War

孙 子 著

袁士槟 译

外语教学与研究出版社

(京)新登字 155 号

京权图字 01-97-1112

图书在版编目(CIP)数据

孙子兵法:汉英对照/(春秋)孙子著;袁士槟译. —北京:外语教学
与研究出版社,1997.12
(大师经典文库)
ISBN 7-5600-1445-3

Ⅰ.孙…　Ⅱ.①孙…②袁…　Ⅲ.孙子兵法-对照读物-汉、英
Ⅳ.H319.4:E

中国版本图书馆 CIP 数据核字(98)第 10961 号

大师经典文库

孙子兵法

孙　子　著
袁士槟　译

* * *

外语教学与研究出版社出版发行
(北京西三环北路 19 号)
http://www.fltrp.com.cn
北京外国语大学印刷厂印刷
开本 850×1168　1/32　2.5 印张
1998 年 7 月第 1 版　1999 年 4 月第 2 次印刷
印数:20001—30000 册

* * *

ISBN 7-5600-1445-3
H·814
定价:3.90 元

出版说明

外语教学与研究出版社自90年代以来，一直以促进国际文化交流为己任，致力于原版外语著作的引进、出版工作，逐步形成了规模化、系统化、精品化的出版传统，在广大读者中产生了一定的影响。当下，我国外语图书出版呈现出较为严重的不均衡局面，即文艺类图书品种相对齐全，而人文科学、社会科学类图书的出版却寥寥可数，远远滞后于日益增长的文化市场需求。为了填补这一空白，外研社决定编辑出版英文版哲学、社会科学类丛书"大师经典文库"，系统地推出一批世界著名思想家、哲学家、政治学家、历史学家、心理学家的经典学术名著，包括我国古代哲学典籍的权威英译本，为广大英语学习者提供高质量的阅读文本，也为各类社会科学研究工作者提供必备的学术资料。本丛书内容详实，制作精美，每一种均约请著名专家、学者专门撰写评介性的序言。外研社将本丛书的出版视做一项利国利民的文化基础工程，将坚持不懈地完善、充实它，希望它能够赢得读者朋友们的喜爱。

外语教学与研究出版社
1997年11月

序　言

张文儒

　　《孙子兵法》是中国古代一部著名兵法，相传为先秦时的大军事家孙武所著。这部兵法，已被世界各国公认为是最富哲理性和发生着深远影响的兵法。凡读过这部兵法的人，不仅会感觉到其有一种独抵华屋之下、一览群小的气度，而且还会倾心仰慕它所蕴含的深邃而奥秘的思辨内容，博大而精深的军事学说内涵，清新而鲜明的实践风格，以及辞如珠玉的文学性语言。其问世虽已有两千五百年之久，但它因为所包容的一些哲学思维，以及在这些哲学文化意识指导下所阐述的战争规律和原则，至今仍然闪烁着熠熠光辉，被称为令人叹为观止的罕世之作，绝非偶然。

　　那么，《孙子兵法》的作者孙武究竟是怎样一个人，我们不妨先作些介绍。

　　孙武即孙子或孙武子，他姓孙名武，字长卿，春秋末期人。其活动年月与著名思想家孔子相仿。孔子生活的年代是公元前551年至479年，而孙武的出生年月据推算在公元前550年至公元前540年之间。

　　孙武的祖籍是春秋时一个小国陈国，位置在现今的河南与安徽的交界处。他的七世先祖陈完本是该国国君陈厉公的儿子，由于宫庭内部发生内讧，陈完怕祸及自身，逃难到齐。其时齐国由桓公当政，封陈完为工正，即掌管齐国手工业生产。这时的陈完改姓田，原因是陈与田音同意通。及至田完的四世孙无宇时，生有二子，一为恒，一为书。田书被当时齐国君主齐景公派往讨伐齐国的邻国莒国，立有战功，被皇室赐姓孙，食采于乐安（一说今山东省惠民县①）。由此，孙氏一家成为了军事世家。孙武的父亲叫孙凭，孙凭乃孙书之子。此时，由于齐国发生内乱，他为

---

① 关于孙武的故里主要有两种见解：一是山东省惠民县，一是山东省博兴县，无定论。本文从前说。

避祸乱，率全家到了南方的吴国。这时的孙武只有二十余岁，但钻研兵法颇有成就。他藏形而不露，过着亦耕亦读的田园生活。

相传，中国原始社会末期中原部族联盟首领舜，曾是陈国人的祖先，孙武也被视为舜的后裔。《吴越春秋》里记载，孙武发怒时，"两目忽张，声如骇虎，发上冲冠，项旁亦缨。"可见其眼睛不小，声音洪亮，体魄健壮，满头乌黑硬发，是一位标准的山东大汉。他的性格内向、耿直，语言明快，思想深刻。

孙武到吴国后，被由楚国逃亡至此的伍子胥发现，并引为知己。伍子胥成为吴王阖闾的谋臣后，曾在吴王面前七次举荐孙武。获准后，吴王令孙武携兵书来见，对他的兵学见解至为赏识。吴王征得孙武同意，派180名宫女给他，以作为练兵示范。孙武受命后，将宫女们分为两队，又选派吴王宠爱的两位妃子为队长，并要呈王派出执掌军法的人和几个助手，以壮军威。当宫女们披挂停当、手持武器、进到操场后，孙武在指挥台上，认真宣讲操练要领。他问道："你们都知道自己的前心、后背和左右手吧?"众宫女觉得问得可笑，便心不在焉地回答："知——道。"孙武接着讲："既知道，一切行动，以鼓为准，命令向前，目视前方；向左，视左手；向右，视右手；向后，指背后，不许吵闹、嬉笑和故意违反军令。"宣讲完毕后，开始操练。一阵击鼓后，宫女们或坐或站，参差不齐。孙武又大声把命令重复一遍，再次击鼓，宫女们依然漫不经心，有些甚至捧腹大笑。孙武大怒，说："口令不清，乃将之过；口令已清，而不去执行，乃士兵的罪过。"说罢，不顾吴王求情，当众斩掉两名队长。自此后，令行禁止，军纪肃然，再也无人敢把操练当儿戏了。这便是史书上有名的"吴宫教战"。

此次操场教练，虽说吴王失去两名爱姬，心中有所不悦，欲辞退孙武，但经过伍子胥一再地晓之以利弊，吴王回心转意，确认孙武是一位既能垂篇史绩、又能实地征战的安邦定国的奇才，遂封孙武为上将军，令他日夜练兵，准备伐楚。

楚国是春秋时期的南方大国，吞并的诸侯国很多，又有北上问鼎中原的趋向，北方的晋国想联吴制楚，使吴楚两国长期对峙。

自吴王阖闾时起,吴国与楚国几次交兵,也深刻认识到:"巩固东南,必争江汉;恢复中原,必得淮泗。"因此,决意与楚国疆场一试。本来,楚国自恃兵力强大,不把吴国放在眼里,但在公元前5世纪楚昭王即位后,有江河日下的趋势,而且又同周边国家如唐、蔡等国,关系搞得很僵,动辄以兵戎相加。吴国利用楚国内忧外患的时机,打着"兴师救蔡"的旗号,逼楚军回防。孙武与伍子胥等率水师溯淮河西上,经蔡,北绕大别山,会唐、蔡军。当吴、蔡、唐三国联军编制就绪后,孙武突然决定改变沿淮水进军的路线,在今河南潢川北,也就是淮河某弯曲部位,舍舟登陆,迅即通过大别山与桐柏山之间的黄岘关、武胜关、平靖关三道关口,直插楚国纵深。

孙武之所以选择为对方料想不到的路线,就是为麻痹对方,打他一个措手不及;同时也体现了兵贵神速,动作迅猛。果然,当联军主力集结在湖北麻城东北柏子山一带后,楚军仓促应战,经过前哨战和柏举决战后,楚军大败。吴军乘胜追击,十一天行军七百里,五战五捷,占领楚国都城郢。楚昭王弃城南逃,吴军则声威大振。这次战役中,吴军以三万人对楚军二十万,出征千里之外,竟取得辉煌战绩,令人们不胜感叹。战国时期军事家尉缭子赞赏说:"有提十万之众,而天下莫当者谁?曰桓公①也。有提七万之众,而天下莫当者谁?曰吴起也。有提三万之众,而天下莫当者谁?曰武子②也。"可见对孙武用兵之神推崇备至;近人历史学家范文澜先生也把柏举战役称作"东周时期第一大战争"。③

从上面介绍的孙武生平和他主要的军事业绩中,已经知道他是一位旷世稀才;然而,更引人注目的,却是他贡献于世的不朽名著——《孙子兵法》。

这部兵法共十三章,约六千余字,但言简意赅,回味无穷,正可谓字字千钧,掷地有声。它从始计开始,到用间结束,把用

---

① 指齐桓公。
② 指孙武。
③ 范文澜:《中国通史简编》修订本,第一篇,第170页。

兵中的各个侧面,各个环节,论述得细密而周全。特别是由于它使用"舍事而言理"的叙述方式,将战争中的计与战、力与智、利与害、全与破、迂与直、数与胜等等相互冲突又相互联结的辩证关系,分析得鞭辟入理,更处处显示出它特有的哲理之光。它的"兵之情主速","攻其无备,出其不意","多算胜,少算不胜","知彼知己者,百战不殆","兵无常势,水无常形",乃至"齐勇若一","吴越同舟","不战而屈人之兵"等,更成为家喻户晓、人人皆知的名言粹语,为古今中外之千万人所传诵。此部兵书真可谓寓意深邃,魅力无穷。

《孙子兵法》先是在国内广为流传。据韩非子《五蠹》记载,战国时,"藏孙吴之书者家有之"。事实上,《战国策》、《尉缭子》、《吕氏春秋》、《荀子》、《淮南子》等书里,对《孙子兵法》也多有征引。三国时的诸葛亮,盛赞孙子的高超计谋,说过:"曹操智计,殊绝于人,其用兵也,仿佛孙吴。"① 这里的孙指孙子,吴指吴起,孙子排在第一。曹操本人为《孙子兵法》作注时,也有不同凡响的见解。他说:"吾观兵书战策多矣,孙武所著深矣。"② 即是指孙子的许多论断已深入到军事行动的精髓,也就是谋略。唐代李世民与他的名将李靖问对时也赞赏说:"观诸兵书,无出孙武。"他特别推崇孙子特有的观察问题的方法及权衡利弊的能力。明代武官兼学者茅元仪更是把《孙子兵法》看作是中国武经之纲。他说:"前孙子者,孙子不遗;后孙子者,不能遗孙子。"③ 将这部兵书在兵学史上的地位阐述得简练而准确。

从国外说,《孙子兵法》也产生了难以估量的影响。自公元8世纪(中国唐代),该书被日本在中国的一位留学生吉备真备带回日本后,这部兵书便越出了国界。公元15世纪,兵法传到朝鲜(李成桂王朝)。公元17世纪时,日本研究《孙子》的著作不下170本,代表作如山鹿素行的《孙子谚义》,著名武将武田信

---

① 《诸葛亮集》,中华书局1960年版,第7
② 《曹操集·孙子序》,中华书局1974年版。
③ 《武备志·兵诀评·序》。

玄的《风、林、火、山——孙子的旗帜》。1905年日俄战争中,日本陆军将领乃木希典应用《孙子兵法》中"以逸待劳"、"以饱待饥"的名言,战胜俄军。取胜后,他以私费出版《孙子谚义》,赠送友人。1772年,一位叫阿米奥的神甫把《孙子》带回法国,在巴黎有了第一个法译本。此书受到拿破仑的青睐,他特别赏识书中说的"施无法之赏,悬无政之令",[①]并在率兵作战中信赏信罚,破格提升许多有胆有识之士,满足下属的功名心态。1860年有俄译本。紧接着,德、意、捷、越、希伯来、罗马尼亚等各种文本相继问世。

二次战后,《孙子兵法》不胫而走,许多国家的著名军事家与杰出的学者都越来越推崇它的谋略学的价值。俄国著名学者E·A·拉津教授说:孙子"在古代中国军事理论思想发展中所起的作用之大,相当于古代世界的亚里士多德在许多领域发展的知识"。[②] 英国功勋卓著的军事家、元帅蒙哥马利也说:世界上所有的军事学院都应把《孙子兵法》列为必修课程。[③]与此同时,翻译和出版有关孙子的书也纷至沓来。继美国退休准将格里菲斯的《孙子》新译本问世之后,接连推出的有阿多俊介的《孙子之新研究》、佐藤坚司的《孙子思想史的研究》等。有学者统计,从本世纪起,仅西方世界,便出现过《孙子兵法》的七个英译本。又据统计,迄至1992年12月底为止,全球出版的《孙子兵法》已有29种文字的版本,其中国内6种,国外23种,包括坦桑尼亚的斯瓦希利语和印度的泰米尔语等稀有语种。《孙子兵法》在传播过程中还有一个特点也应看到。它虽说是兵书,但由于其思想深刻、涵盖面广,已获得普遍认同;其影响所至,已远远超出军事,变成指导经济、政治、文化、外交、体育乃至人生的各个方面的不朽经典。美国著名的兰德公司学者波拉克说得对:孙子和孔子一样有永恒的智慧,这种智慧属于全世界,没有哪个国家能够垄断。

《孙子兵法》之所以会产生如此广泛而深远的影响,是和这

---

① 语出《孙子兵法·九地篇》。
②③ 引自《孙子新探——中外学者论孙子》,第334、326页。

部书反映的哲学思维的特点及文化内涵分不开的。

从哲学思维的特点看,《孙子兵法》表现了朴素的唯物观点与辩证法,因而能高屋建瓴,驾驭全局。

孙武认为,战争有客观的法则,这些法则可以被认识,因而,战争双方的胜负也可以预知。这些法则究竟是借助于哪些条件而起作用的呢?他提出道、天、地、将、法五条。首先是统治者决策时必须使老百姓和他的意志一致,"令民与上同意"("道")。其次是有利的天候即气象条件("天")。其次是便于作战的地形地貌和有利的地理位置("地")。其次是有善于指挥作战的将领("将")。其次是有良好的军事纪律及充分的后勤供应("法")。假若这五方面都胜过对方,便可以兴兵作战,有取胜把握;假如其中一项或两项不合乎要求,又没有相应的补偿办法,便不应发兵,即使发兵也难以取胜。

一般说来,人们对自己一方的情况较为熟识,而对方的情况便若明若暗,怎样超越这一障碍呢?孙子认为应取决于人,就是派间谍了解对方真实情况。他说过:"以故明君贤将所以动而胜人,成功出于众者,先知也。先知者,不可取于鬼神,不可象于事(以过去相似的事物作类比),不可验于度(以日月星辰运行的位置来占卜吉凶祸福),必取于人,知敌之情者也。"[①] 他告诫人们,既不要相信天命,也不要相信鬼神,要靠能了解真实情况的活着的人。这里鲜明地反映了他的看法:天地之间,人为贵。

依据孙武的上述见解,他作出结论:了解敌人又了解自己,百战都不会失败;不了解敌人而了解自己,胜败的可能各半;既不了解敌人,又不了解自己,那就每战必败("故曰:知彼知己者,百战不殆;不知彼而知己,一胜一负;不知彼,不知己,每战必殆"[②])。

不过,需要说明的是:在孙子看来,全面地了解敌我双方情况,只是提供了战争中取胜的必要条件,尚不是充分条件。如要最终取胜,还须对了解来的实际情况,进行"察"(考察、研

---

① 《孙子兵法·用间篇》。
② 《孙子兵法·谋攻篇》。

究)、"算"（计算、谋划），形成具体的战略、战术，并在行动中力求创造出使自己不被敌人战胜的条件，然后才谈得上战胜对方。这里的"察"和"算"都要有上乘的思维方式辅助进行，也就是运用辩证思维。

何为辩证思维？就是把考察对象看成活生生的、运动变化的、相互联结而又彼此对立的东西，而不是刻板固定的死的东西。从《孙子兵法》里看出，它把战争这种现象看作如自然现象和其它社会现象一样，不是静止不动的，是处在不断的运动变化当中；而且，战争中的变动表现得更加迅速和剧烈。在谈到自然界的变化时，孙子说过"四时无常胜，五行无常位，日有短长，月有死生"。[①]谈到战争时，他则说："乱生于治，怯生于勇，弱生于强。"[②]

既然战争是变化万端、难以把握的，那么，从事战争的人，无论国君或将帅也必须适应于这种变化，善于将变与不变巧妙结合起来，取胜对方。孙子说过："声不过五，五声之变，不可胜听也。色不过五，五色之变，不可胜观也。味不过五，五味之变，不可胜尝也。战势不过奇正，奇正之变，不可胜穷也。"[③]这里说的正是正规，奇指奇变，认为两者可相机使用或交替运用。书中谈到指挥战争的人要把战争原则灵活运用时又说："兵无常势，水无常形。能因敌变化而取胜者谓之神。"[④]

正是本着对战争这一事物的辩证思考，《孙子兵法》里将战争中经常出现的矛盾现象，如敌我、彼己、主客、动静、进退、攻守、速久、虚实、奇正、专分、利害、安危、险易、广狭、远近、众寡、劳逸、强弱、胜败等，均作了妥贴的和精当的分析，这成为《孙子兵法》里极具思辩特色的内容。

《孙子兵法》所体现的人文睿智集中地表现在它的高超谋略。

什么是谋略，简言之是智谋与方略，即在广博知识的基础上，凭借于思维能力的超常发挥而铸就的深谋远虑的本领。假如讲详

---

① 《孙子兵法·军争篇》
②③ 《孙子兵法·势篇》
④ 《孙子兵法·虚实篇》

细一点，就是指人在认识对象时，善于从总体与部分、表层与里层、长远与短暂、实体与环境、预知因素与随机因素等各个方面作细致的分析，通过比较与权衡，尽快作出合乎实际的精当决断，并以少得多得为原则，提出相应的行动规划与计划。如人们所熟知的，由于战争是激烈的对抗行为，参战双方往往在限定的时间与地域，倾其所有物质力量与精神力量，进行全方位的生死较量，它理当成为谋略学最初的发源地；而《孙子兵法》作为一本最上乘的军事哲学著作，它所提供的谋略内容也必然成为其中最关键和最核心的组成部分。书中说的"兵者诡道"、"多算胜"、"上兵伐谋"，便是包含丰富谋略遗产的有力佐证。

　　从前面介绍的《孙子兵法》在国内与国外的传播过程中，人们也许会发现：由于历史条件及人的认识能力的限制，这部兵法里最先受到重视的，还不是谋略内容，而是某些战术原则和用兵技巧。无论是《战国策》、《尉缭子》、《吕氏春秋》，还是《淮南子》，大多是征引、复述孙子贡献的某些战术，如兵贵神速、兵不厌诈，而较少涉及军事谋略。只是汉代的任宏在将兵书分类时，才把兵书内容分为兵权谋、兵形势、兵阴阳、兵技巧四类。他说的兵权谋与现在说的谋略含义相近，只是没有对《孙子兵法》里的各项谋略细加发挥，而到三国时期的诸葛亮和曹操，则更多地将注意力集中于孙子提供的高超智谋，认为书中的许多论断已经深入军事行动的精髓，闪烁着人类智慧的火花。国外的传播状况也大体类似，日本战国末年的著名武将武田信玄(1511－1573)曾特别挑选出《孙子兵法·军争篇》里的四句话："其疾如风，其徐如林，侵掠如火，不动如山，"并把每句话的最后一个字合在一起，成为"风林火山"，用大字绣在军旗上，以醒耳目并振奋军威。但这里只涉及战术原则，而到法国拿破仑时代便有不同。拿破仑所赏识的孙子主张过的法外之赏及政外之令，便含有打破常轨和运用奇变的方法去选拔培养人才和从事作战的意思，把奇与变上升到谋略高度。拿破仑在率军作战中，正是以惯走出人意外的行军路线和在治军中破格选拔优秀人才而逐步改变其不利态势的。尤其是他重用人才，成为他得以改变军队上层领导成分，剔除群雄，一时巍然君临全欧、战功赫赫的重要因素。

本世纪40年代，二次大战接近结束和核武器君临人世以来，几乎全球每一个国家甚至每一个人都认识到，自己难逃核战争的劫难；与此同时，由于生产力的飞跃发展，战争的规模、形式以及作战方式都与以往不可同日而语。这样，《孙子兵法》里谈到的具体战术原则和统兵技巧，有些已显得过时，有些降低了价值；与此相反，其所提供的战略思考，则在明显地升值。美国历史学家莫里斯·马特洛夫博士曾说过这样的话，他说："在20世纪进行战略抉择从来就不是一件容易的事情，而且，自第二次世界大战结束以来，在这个动荡不安的世界上进行战略抉择更是事关重大。"① 《孙子兵法》所提供的正是高超的智谋。

让我们看一看美国的外层空间防御计划(即星球大战计划)，对孙子谋略的重要位置就一目了然了。

人们知道，在战后几十年全球两极对峙的格局之下，双方都曾把"确保摧毁对方"作为终极目标。不幸的是，在这一思路下面，出现了为双方非始料所及的局面，核武器愈积愈多，杀伤力愈来愈强；及至最后，竞赛双方中任何一方都没有把握能在不遭受对方核报复的条件下将对方"摧毁"。因为武器进步到如此程度：用洲际导弹射击几千里以外的目标，只允许有30分钟报警和还击的时间，稍有差错，被打击的地方就会变为一片焦土，尔后还得面对核冬天带来的无穷祸患。很显然，人们所面临的严峻现实是："相互确保摧毁"所提供的战略选择决非是明智的；即使排除偶然的意外，设定双方决策人物都十分理智地行事，也无异于是把对方的亿万人生命当作赌注，或当作人质，以求实施自己的战略目的。这不仅违背人道主义而在舆论上受到强烈的谴责，而且事实上也会由于两败俱伤而不能达到自己的目的。

在这样的背景下，另一条思路应运而生，即不是先保证摧毁对手，而且是先确保自己生存。按照这条新的思路，问题的关节不在进攻而在防御，即先设法把自己置于不败之地。1983年3月

---

① 美国陆军军事学院编：《军事战略》中译本，第39页。

23日美国总统里根发表的以制定美国弹道导弹防御计划为内容的电视讲话作为标志，反映了这一战略转折的开始。依据这一计划，在未来数十年内，美国将大力修造一座"太空盾"，即以各种型号的外层空间站为据点，对外来导弹的攻击实行空间的多层拦截，使真正落在地面上的核杀伤力变得微乎其微。

人们一定会问：这种高超的谋略，其最初的源头出自何人之手？关于这一点，许多学者几乎异口同声地认为：它的起源是中国的孙武。正是《孙子兵法》贡献出了这样一种卓越的谋略：百战百胜，不算是好中最好的；不动用武力而使对方屈服，才算是好中最好的（"是故百战百胜，非善之善者也；不战而屈人之兵，善之善者也"①）。孙子又说：用兵的法则，不要寄希望于敌人不会来，而要自己严阵以待；不要寄希望于敌人不会进攻，而要准备好使对方无法破坏也无法取胜的充足力量（"故用兵之法，无恃其不来，恃吾有以待也；无恃其不攻，恃吾有所不可攻也"②）。这两段话，几乎一字不差地可以为上述的外层空间防御的构思作注脚。难怪美国陆军上校小阿瑟·莱克著文赞赏说：孙子所论述的问题都关系到战争的基本原理和原则，因此他的军事思想虽产生于公元前5世纪，今天却仍很适用。③

事实上，由于《孙子兵法》里的谋略内容体现了人类智慧的结晶，其适用范围已不限于某一社会活动领域，除军事谋略外，又延伸为政治谋略、经济谋略、外交谋略、统御谋略、说辩谋略等。

以上介绍的是《孙子兵法》中包含的哲学智慧与人文内涵，下面再谈谈它与现代科学方法论的相同或相似之处。

现代科学方法论是随着人类活动范围的拓展及各门科学的进步，以及人的认识能力的升华而被提炼出来的一种适合于现代人的认识工具。它包容有多方面内容，而且，其内容还在继续扩展与丰富。但这并不是说，在古代人的认识中不包含现代科学方法的胚胎或萌芽。恰恰相反，由于中国人在先秦时代，其抽象思维

---

①② 《孙子兵法·谋攻篇》。
③ 参见美国陆军军事学院编：《军事战略》中译本，第15页。

能力已达到相当高的水平，因而在他们的著作中不难找出现代人认识的雏形。具体来说，《孙子兵法》里有过系统科学与心理学的幼芽。

现代系统科学方法要求有系统性思维和优化选择，要求在决策前对各种可行性方案作科学论证，经过比较和选择定出最佳方案。《孙子兵法》里虽没有使用过系统这一概念，但其每一处的论证，无不在字里行间闪烁着系统思维的光辉。例如，在《计篇》里，他举出军事系统里五种相关要素是道、天、地、将、法；在《形篇》里，当分析到一个国家的战争能力与潜力究竟有多大时，他捉住了度、量、数、称、胜五个关节；当分析到一位将领应具备哪些基本素质时，他又举出智、信、仁、勇、严五项；当分析间谍的类型时，他还提出它包括因间（乡间）、内间、反间、死间、生间五类；在《地形篇》和《九变篇》里，他分别提出了兵有六败，将有五危，即用兵不当，有五种情况要失败，主将不力，有五种情况很危险。所有这些，都表现了孙武在分析战争问题时，极善于从其各个侧面作整体分析或系统分析，并通过这些相关要素的分析与估算，去推断战争的未来与结局。否则，一切超前推断都无从谈起。反过来，如果想提高战争中一方的整体作战能力，也必须把注意力放在构筑一个合乎规格的稳定的统一体上面，注重于统一体内部各个要素的自身素质及它们间的相互协调，单打一的做法对指导战争有百害而无一利。

《孙子兵法》里对于人的心理分析也很突出，也就是着重于研究某一个体或群体在特定的社会生活条件下或处于特殊环境时，心理活动与心理态势变化的规律。

例如，书中分析说：君有三患，一是不了解军队该不该前进或后退而贸然作出决定；二是不熟悉军队的内部管理办法而盲目干涉下属的行政事务；三是不懂得权谋而给部下乱出主意。这三种祸患都是由于君主自以为身处高位便全智全能。孙子认为，这是一种极不正常的心理态势，须时刻加以防范。

他又分析说，作为将领也有一些性格上的弱点很危险，如过分地自信、懦弱及优柔寡断等，特别是当将帅和士卒心理态势不统一时往往招致战争的失败。他举例说：有的部队里士卒强悍而将吏懦弱，上级难以对部下统帅约束，致使军政废弛而失败，叫做"弛"；又有些队伍里，主将极有主见，命令业已下达，但部下不理解主将意图，不服从指挥，怨怒之余又自行出战，叫做"崩"。诸如此类，都告诉人们：做一名将帅，如不从根本上改善自己的心理素质和心理态势，难以成为合格将领，更不必说去统兵御敌。

对于士兵，《孙子兵法》里也有过细的心理分析。他说，士兵也与常人一样，有七情六欲，有极细微的心理活动，他们需要悉心关怀，但又必须严格训练。如果将帅对待士兵能像对待婴儿一样体贴，士兵就肯于跟随将帅去赴汤蹈火；将帅对士兵如能像对自己的"爱子"一样，士兵就可以与将帅同生共死。但是，关怀与爱护都要适度，假若对其过分厚养而不能使用，一味溺爱而不能令使，违反了纪律也不严肃处理，这样的军队，好比"骄子"一样，是不能用来打仗的（"厚而不能使，爱而不能令，乱而不能治，譬若骄子，不可用也"）。①

现代战争的史实已经证明：心理因素所起的作用往往大于物理因素，如果在一场大的战争中，能把精神的或心理的要素置于恰当地位，不但能补偿一部分物质力量的不足，还往往对整个战局产生决定性的影响。

勿庸讳言，当今世界，重视人的心理因素，不但战争中适用，对其它如政治、外交、体育、商贸等领域也无不适用。

---

① 《孙子兵法·地形篇》。

孙子兵法

The Art of War

始计第一

孙子曰：兵者，国之大事，死生之地，存亡之道，不可不察也。

故经之以五事，校之以计，而索其情：一曰道，二曰天，三曰地，四曰将，五曰法。道者，令民与上同意也，故可以与之死，可以与之生，而不畏危。天者，阴阳、寒暑、时制也。地者，远近、险易、广狭、死生也。将者，智、信、仁、勇、严也。法者，曲制、管道、主用也。

凡此五者，将莫不闻，知之者胜，不知者不胜。故校之以计。而索其情。

曰：主孰有道?将孰有能?天地孰得?法令孰行?兵众孰强?士卒孰练?赏罚孰明?

吾以此知胜负矣。

将听吾计，用之必胜，留之；将不听吾计，用之必败，去之。

计利以听，乃为之势，以佐其外。势者，因利而制权也。

兵者，诡道也。故能而示之不能，用而示之不用，近而示之远，远而示之近。利而诱之，乱而取之，实而备之，强而避之，怒而挠之，卑而骄之，佚而劳之，亲而离之。攻其无备，出其不意。此兵家之胜，不可先传也。

　　夫未战而庙算胜者，得算多也；未战而庙算不胜者，得算少也。多算胜，少算不胜，而况于无算乎?吾以此观之，胜负见矣。

CHAPTER 1

Estimates

War is a matter of vital importance to the state; a matter of life or death, the road either to survival or to ruin. Hence, it is imperative that it be studied thoroughly.

Therefore, appraise it in terms of the five fundamental factors and make comparisons of the various conditions of the antagonistic sides in order to ascertain the results of a war. The first of these factors is politics; the second, weather; the third, terrain; the fourth, the commander; and the fifth, doctrine. Politics means the thing which causes the people to be in harmony with their ruler so that they will follow him in disregard of their lives and without fear of any danger. Weather signifies night and day, cold and heat, fine days and rain, and change of seasons. Terrain means distances, and refers to whether the ground is traversed with ease or difficulty and to whether it is open or constricted, and influences your chances of life or death. The commander stands for the general's qualities of wisdom, sincerity, benevolence, courage, and strictness. Doctrine is to be understood as the organisation of the army, the gradations of rank among the officers, the regulation of supply routes, and the provision of military materials to the army.

These five fundamental factors are familiar to every general. Those who master them win; those who do not are defeated. Therefore, in laying plans, compare the following seven elements, appraising them with the utmost care.

1 Which ruler is wise and more able?
2 Which commander is more talented?
3 Which army obtains the advantages of nature and the terrain?
4 In which army are regulations and instructions better carried out?
5 Which troops are stronger?

6 Which army has the better-trained officers and men?
7 Which army administers rewards and punishments in a more enlightened and correct way?

By means of these seven elements, I shall be able to forecast which side will be victorious and which will be defeated.

The general who heeds my counsel is sure to win. Such a general should be retained in command. One who ignores my counsel is certain to be defeated. Such a one should be dismissed.

Having paid attention to my counsel and plans, the general must create a situation which will contribute to their accomplishment. By 'situation' I mean he should take the field situation into consideration and act in accordance with what is advantageous.

All warfare is based on deception. Therefore, when capable of attacking, feign incapacity; when active in moving troops, feign inactivity. When near the enemy, make it seem that you are far away; when far away, make it seem that you are near. Hold out baits to lure the enemy. Strike the enemy when he is in disorder. Prepare against the enemy when he is secure at all points. Avoid the enemy for the time being when he is stronger. If your opponent is of choleric temper, try to irritate him. If he is arrogant, try to encourage his egotism. If the enemy troops are well prepared after reorganisation, try to wear them down. If they are united, try to sow dissension among them. Attack the enemy where he is unprepared, and appear where you are not expected. These are the keys to victory for a strategist. It is not possible to formulate them in detail beforehand.

Now, if the estimates made before a battle indicate victory, it is because careful calculations show that your conditions are more favourable than those of your enemy; if they indicate defeat, it is because careful calculations show that favourable conditions for a battle are fewer. With more careful calculations, one can win; with less, one cannot. How much less chance of victory has one who makes no calculations at all! By this means, one can foresee the outcome of a battle.

作战第二

孙子曰：凡用兵之法，驰车千驷，革车千乘，带甲十万，千里馈粮，则内外之费，宾客之用，胶漆之材，车甲之奉，日费千金，然后十万之师举矣。

其用战也胜，久则钝兵挫锐，攻城则力屈，久暴师则国用不足。夫钝兵挫锐，屈力殚货，则诸侯乘其弊而起，虽有智者，不能善其后矣。故兵闻拙速，未睹巧之久也。夫兵久而国利者，未之有也。故不尽知用兵之害者，则不能尽知用兵之利也。

善用兵者，役不再籍，粮不三载；取用于国，因粮于敌，故军食可足也。

国之贫于师者远输，远输则百姓贫。近于师者贵卖，贵卖则百姓财竭，财竭则急于丘役。力屈、财殚，中原内虚于家。百姓之费，十去其七；公家之费，破车罢马，甲胄矢弩，戟盾蔽橹，丘牛大车，十去其六。

故智将务食于敌，食敌一钟，当吾二十钟；萁秆一石，当吾二十石。

故杀敌者，怒也；取敌之利者，货也。

故车战，得车十乘已上，赏其先得者，而更其旌旗，车杂而乘之，卒善而养之，是谓胜敌而益强。

故兵贵胜，不贵久。故知兵之将，生民之司命，国家安危之主也。

CHAPTER 2

Waging War

In operations of war – when one thousand fast four-horse chariots, one thousand heavy chariots, and one thousand mail-clad soldiers are required; when provisions are transported for a thousand *li*; when there are expenditures at home and at the front, and stipends for entertainment of envoys and advisers – the cost of materials such as glue and lacquer, and of chariots and armour, will amount to one thousand pieces of gold a day. One hundred thousand troops may be dispatched only when this money is in hand.

A speedy victory is the main object in war. If this is long in coming, weapons are blunted and morale depressed. If troops are attacking cities, their strength will be exhausted. When the army engages in protracted campaigns, the resources of the state will fall short. When your weapons are dulled and ardour dampened, your strength exhausted and treasure spent, the chieftains of the neighbouring states will take advantage of your crisis to act. In that case, no man, however wise, will be able to avert the disastrous consequences that ensue. Thus, while we have heard of stupid haste in war, we have not yet seen a clever operation that was prolonged. For there has never been a protracted war which benefited a country. Therefore, those unable to understand the evils inherent in employing troops are equally unable to understand the advantageous ways of doing so.

Those adept in waging war do not require a second levy of conscripts or more than two provisionings. They carry military equipment from the homeland, but rely on the enemy for provisions. Thus, the army is plentifully provided with food.

When a country is impoverished by military operations, it is due to distant transportation; carrying supplies for great distances renders the people destitute. Where troops are gathered, prices go up. When prices rise, the wealth of the people is drained away. When wealth is drained away, the people will be afflicted with urgent and heavy exactions. With this loss of wealth and exhaustion of strength the households in the country will be extremely poor and seven-tenths of their wealth dissipated. As to government expenditures, those due to broken-down chariots, worn-out horses, armour and helmets, bows and arrows, spears and shields, protective mantlets, draft oxen, and wagons will amount to 60 percent of the total.

Hence, a wise general sees to it that his troops feed on the enemy, for one *zhong* of the enemy's provisions is equivalent to twenty of one's own and one *shi* of the enemy's fodder to twenty *shi* of one's own.

In order to make the soldiers courageous in overcoming the enemy, they must be roused to anger. In order to capture more booty from the enemy, soldiers must have their rewards.

Therefore, in chariot fighting when more than ten chariots are captured, reward those who take the first. Replace the enemy's flags and banners with your own, mix the captured chariots with yours, and mount them. Treat the prisoners of war well, and care for them. This is called 'winning a battle and becoming stronger'.

Hence, what is valued in war is victory, not prolonged operations. And the general who understands how to employ troops is the minister of the people's fate and arbiter of the nation's destiny.

谋攻第三

孙子曰：凡用兵之法，全国为上，破国次之；全军为上，破军次之；全旅为上，破旅次之；全卒为上，破卒次之；全伍为上，破伍次之。是故百战百胜，非善之善者也；不战而屈人之兵，善之善者也。

故上兵伐谋，其次伐交，其次伐兵，其下攻城。攻城之法为不得已。修橹轒辒，具器械，三月而后成，距闉，又三月而后已。将不胜其忿，而蚁附之，杀士三分之一，而城不拔者，此攻之灾也。

故善用兵者，屈人之兵而非战也，拔人之城而非攻也，毁人之国而非久也，必以全争于天下，故兵不顿，而利可全，此谋攻之法也。

故用兵之法，十则围之，五则攻之，倍则分之，敌则能战之，少则能逃之，不若则能避之。故小敌之坚，大敌之擒也。

夫将者，国之辅也，辅周则国必强，辅隙则国必弱。

故君之所以患于军者三：不知军之不可以进而谓之进，不知军之不可以退而谓之退，是谓縻军；不知三军之事而同三军之政者，则军士惑矣；不知三军之权而同三军之任，则军士疑矣。

三军既惑且疑，则诸侯之难至矣，是谓乱军引胜。

故知胜有五：知可以战与不可以战者胜，识众寡之用者胜，上下同欲者胜，以虞待不虞者胜，将能而君不御者胜。

此五者，知胜之道也。

故曰：知彼知己，百战不殆；不知彼而知己，一胜一负；不知彼，不知己，每战必殆。

CHAPTER 3

Offensive Strategy

Generally, in war the best policy is to take a state intact; to ruin it is inferior to this. To capture the enemy's entire army is better than to destroy it; to take intact a regiment, a company, or a squad is better than to destroy them. [Regiment, company, and squad are *lu*, *zu*, and *wu* in Chinese. In ancient China, five hundred soldiers made up a *lu*, one hundred a *zu*, and five a *wu*.] For to win one hundred victories in one hundred battles is not the acme of skill. To subdue the enemy without fighting is the supreme excellence.

Thus, what is of supreme importance in war is to attack the enemy's strategy. Next best is to disrupt his alliances by diplomacy. The next best is to attack his army. And the worst policy is to attack cities. Attack cities only when there is no alternative because to prepare big shields and wagons and make ready the necessary arms and equipment require at least three months, and to pile up earthen ramps against the walls requires an additional three months. The general, unable to control his impatience, will order his troops to swarm up the wall like ants, with the result that one-third of them will be killed without taking the city. Such is the calamity of attacking cities.

Thus, those skilled in war subdue the enemy's army without battle. They capture the enemy's cities without assaulting them and overthrow his state without protracted operations. Their aim is to take all under heaven intact by strategic considerations. Thus, their troops are not worn out and their gains will be complete. This is the art of offensive strategy.

Consequently, the art of using troops is this: When ten to the enemy's one, surround him. When five times his strength, attack him. If double his strength, divide him. If equally matched, you may engage him with some good plan. If weaker numerically, be capable of withdrawing. And if in all respects unequal, be capable of eluding him, for a small force is but booty for one more powerful if it fights recklessly.

Now, the general is the assistant to the sovereign of the state. If this assistance is all-embracing, the state will surely be strong; if defective, the state will certainly be weak.

Now, there are three ways in which a sovereign can bring misfortune upon his army:

1 When ignorant that the army should not advance, to order an advance; or when ignorant that it should not retire, to order a retirement. This is described as 'hobbling the army'.
2 When ignorant of military affairs, to interfere in their administration. This causes the officers to be perplexed.
3 When ignorant of command problems, to interfere with the direction of fighting. This engenders doubts in the minds of the officers.

If the army is confused and suspicious, neighbouring rulers will take advantage of this and cause trouble. This is what is meant by: 'A confused army leads to another's victory'.

Thus, there are five points in which victory may be predicted:

1 He who knows when he can fight and when he cannot will be victorious.
2 He who understands how to fight in accordance with the strength of antagonistic forces will be victorious.
3 He whose ranks are united in purpose will be victorious.
4 He who is well prepared and lies in wait for an enemy who is not well prepared will be victorious.
5 He whose generals are able and not interfered with by the sovereign will be victorious.

It is in these five matters that the way to victory is known. Therefore, I say: Know the enemy and know yourself; in a hundred battles, you will never be defeated. When you are ignorant of the enemy but know yourself, your chances of winning or losing are equal. If ignorant both of your enemy and of yourself, you are sure to be defeated in every battle.

军形第四

孙子曰：昔之善战者，先为不可胜，以待敌之可胜。不可胜在己，可胜在敌。故善战者，能为不可胜，不能使敌之可胜。故曰：胜可知，而不可为。

不可胜者，守也；可胜者，攻也。守则不足，攻则有余。善守者，藏于九地之下；善攻者，动于九天之上，故能自保而全胜也。

见胜不过众人之所知，非善之善者也；战胜而天下曰善，非善之善者也。故举秋毫不为多力，见日月不为明目，闻雷霆不为聪耳。古之所谓善战者，胜于易胜者也。故善战者之胜也，无智名，无勇功。故其战胜不忒，不忒者，其所措必胜，胜已败者也。故善战者，立于不败之地，而不失敌之败也。是故胜兵先胜而后求战，败兵先战而后求胜。善用兵者，修道而保法，故能为胜败之政。

兵法：一曰度，二曰量，三曰数，四曰称，五曰胜。地生度，度生量，量生数，数生称，称生胜。故胜兵若以镒称铢，败兵若以铢称镒。

胜者之战，若决积水于千仞之溪者，形也。

CHAPTER 4

Dispositions

The skilful warriors in ancient times first made themselves invincible and then awaited the enemy's moment of vulnerability. Invincibility depends on oneself, but the enemy's vulnerability on himself. It follows that those skilled in war can make themselves invincible but cannot cause an enemy to be certainly vulnerable. Therefore, it can be said that, one may know how to win, but cannot necessarily do so.

Defend yourself when you cannot defeat the enemy, and attack the enemy when you can. One defends when his strength is inadequate; he attacks when it is abundant. Those who are skilled in defence hide themselves as under the ninefold earth; [in ancient China, the number nine was used to signify the highest number.] Those in attack flash forth as from above the ninefold heavens. Thus, they are capable both of protecting themselves and of gaining a complete victory.

To foresee a victory which the ordinary man can foresee is not the acme of excellence. Neither is it if you triumph in battle and are universally acclaimed 'expert', for to lift an autumn down requires no great strength, to distinguish between the sun and moon is no test of vision, to hear the thunderclap is no indication of acute hearing. In ancient times, those called skilled in war conquered an enemy easily conquered. And, therefore, the victories won by a master of war gain him neither reputation for wisdom nor merit for courage. For he wins his victories without erring. Without erring he establishes the certainty of his victory; he conquers an enemy already defeated. Therefore, the skilful commander takes up a position in which he cannot be defeated and misses no opportunity to overcome his enemy. Thus, a victorious army always seeks battle after his plans indicate that victory is possible under them, whereas an army destined to defeat fights in the hope of winning but without any planning. Those skilled in war cultivate their policies and strictly adhere to the laws and regulations. Thus, it is in their power to control success.

Now, the elements of the art of war are first, the measurement of space; second, the estimation of quantities; third, calculations; fourth, comparisons; and fifth, chances of victory. Measurements of space are derived from the ground. Quantities derive from measurement, figures from quantities, comparisons from figures, and victory from comparisons. Thus, a victorious army is as one *yi* [an ancient Chinese weight, approximately equivalent to 24 ounces] balanced against a grain, and a defeated army is as a grain balanced against one *yi*.

It is because of disposition that a victorious general is able to make his soldiers fight with the effect of pent-up waters which, suddenly released, plunge into a bottomless abyss.

兵势第五

孙子曰：凡治众如治寡，分数是也；斗众如斗寡，形名是也；三军之众，可使必受敌而无败者，奇正是也；兵之所加，如以碫投卵者，虚实是也。

凡战者，以正合，以奇胜。故善出奇者，无穷如天地，不竭如江河。终而复始，日月是也。死而复生，四时是也。声不过五，五声之变，不可胜听也。色不过五，五色之变，不可胜观也。味不过五，五味之变，不可胜尝也。战势不过奇正，奇正之变，不可胜穷也。奇正相生，如循环之无端，孰能穷之？

激水之疾，至于漂石者，势也；鸷鸟之疾，至于毁折者，节也。是故善战者，其势险，其节短。势如矿弩，节如发机。

纷纷纭纭，斗乱而不可乱也；浑浑沌沌，形圆而不可败也。乱生于治，怯生于勇，弱生于强。治乱，数也；勇怯，势也；强弱，形也。故善动敌者，形之，敌必从之；予之，敌必取之；以利动之，以卒待之。

故善战者，求之于势，不责于人，故能择人而任势。任势者，其战人也，如转木石。木石之性，安则静，危则动，方则止，圆则行。故善战人之势，如转圆石于千仞之山者，势也。

CHAPTER 5

Posture of Army

Generally management of a large force is the same as management of a few men. It is a matter of organisation. And to direct a large force is the same as to direct a few men. This is a matter of formations and signals. That the army is certain to sustain the enemy's attack without suffering defeat is due to operations of the extraordinary and the normal forces. Troops thrown against the enemy as a grindstone against eggs is an example of a solid acting upon a void.

Generally, in battle, use the normal force to engage and use the extraordinary to win. Now, the resources of those skilled in the use of extraordinary forces are all infinite as the heavens and earth, as inexhaustible as the flow of the great rivers, for they end and recommence – cyclical, as are the movements of the sun and moon. They die away and are reborn – recurrent, as are the passing seasons. The musical notes are only five in number, but their combination gives rise to so numerous melodies that one cannot hear them all. The primary colours are only five in number, but their combinations are so infinite that one cannot visualise them all. The flavours are only five in number, but their blends are so various that one cannot taste them all. In battle, there are only the normal and extraordinary forces, but their combinations are limitless; none can comprehend them all. For these two forces are mutually reproductive. It is like moving in an endless circle. Who can exhaust the possibility of their combination?

When torrential water tosses boulders, it is because of its momentum; when the strike of a hawk breaks the body of its prey, it is because of timing. Thus, the momentum of one skilled in war is overwhelming, and his attack precisely timed. His potential is that of a fully drawn crossbow; his timing, that of the release of the trigger.

In the tumult and uproar, the battle seems chaotic, but there must be no disorder in one's own troops. The battlefield may seem in confusion and chaos, but one's array must be in good order. That will be proof against defeat. Apparent confusion is a product of good order; apparent cowardice, of courage; apparent weakness, of strength. Order or disorder depends on organisation and direction; courage or cowardice on circumstances; strength or weakness on tactical dispositions. Thus, one who is skilled at making the enemy move does so by creating a situation, according to which the enemy will act. He entices the enemy with something he is certain to want. He keeps the enemy on the move by holding out bait and then attacks him with picked troops.

Therefore, a skilled commander seeks victory from the situation and does not demand it of his subordinates. He selects suitable men and exploits the situation. He who utilises the situation uses his men in fighting as one rolls logs or stones. Now, the nature of logs and stones is that on stable ground they are static; on a slope, they move. If square, they stop; if round, they roll. Thus, the energy of troops skilfully commanded in battle may be compared to the momentum of round boulders which roll down from a mountain thousands of feet in height.

虚实第六

孙子曰：凡先处战地而待敌者佚，后处战地而趋战者劳。故善战者，致人而不致于人。能使敌人自至者，利之也；能使敌人不得至者，害之也。故敌佚能劳之，饱能饥之，安能动之。

出其所不趋，趋其所不意。

行千里而不劳者，行于无人之地也。攻而必取者，攻其所不守也；守而必固者，守其所不攻也。故善攻者，敌不知其所守；善守者，敌不知其所攻。

微乎微乎，至于无形；神乎神乎，至于无声，故能为敌之司命。进而不可御者，冲其虚也；退而不可追者，速而不可及也。故我欲战，敌虽高垒深沟，不得不与我战者，攻其所必救也；我不欲战，画地而守之，敌不得与我战者，乖其所之也。

故形人而我无形，则我专而敌分；我专为一，敌分为十，是以十攻其一也，则我众而敌寡；能以众击寡者，则吾之所与战者，约矣。吾所与战之地不可知，不可知，则敌所备者多，敌所备者多，则吾所与战者寡矣。故备前则后寡，备后则前寡，备左则右寡，备右则左寡，无所不备则无所不寡。寡者备人者也，众者使人备己者也。

故知战之地，知战之日，则可千里而会战。不知战地，不知战日，则左不能救右，右不能救左，前不能救后，后不能救前，而况远者数十里，近者数里乎？以吾度之，越人之兵虽多，亦奚益于胜则哉？故曰：胜可为也。敌虽众，可使无斗。

故策之而知得失之计，作之而知动静之理，形之而知死生之地，角之而知有余不足之处。故形兵之极，至于无形；无形，则深间不能窥，智者不能谋。因形而错胜于众，众不能知；人皆知我所以胜之形，而莫知吾所以制胜之形；故其战胜不复，而应形于无穷。

夫兵形象水，水之形避高而趋下，兵之形避实而击虚，水因地而制流，兵因敌而制胜。故兵无常势，水无常形，能因敌变化而取胜者，谓之神。故五行无常胜，四时无常位，日有短长，月有死生。

CHAPTER 6

Void and Actuality

Generally he who occupies the field of battle first and awaits his enemy is at ease, and he who comes later to the scene and rushes into the fight is weary. And, therefore, those skilled in war bring the enemy to the field of battle and are not brought there by him. One able to make the enemy come of his own accord does so by offering him some advantage. And one able to stop him from coming does so by preventing him. Thus, when the enemy is at ease be able to tire him, when well fed to starve him, when at rest to make him move.

Appear at places which he is unable to rescue; move swiftly in a direction where you are least expected.

That you may march a thousand *li* without tiring yourself is because you travel where there is no enemy. To be certain to take what you attack is to attack a place the enemy does not or cannot protect. To be certain to hold what you defend is to defend a place the enemy dares not or is not able to attack. Therefore, against those skilled in attack, the enemy does not know where to defend, and against the experts in defence, the enemy does not know where to attack.

How subtle and insubstantial, that the expert leaves no trace. How divinely mysterious, that he is inaudible. Thus, he is master of his enemy's fate. His offensive will be irresistible if he makes for his enemy's weak positions; he cannot be overtaken when he withdraws if he moves swiftly. When I wish to give battle, my enemy, even though protected by high walls and deep moats, cannot help but engage me, for I attack a position he must relieve. When I wish to avoid battle, I may defend myself simply by drawing a line on the ground; the enemy will be unable to attack me because I divert him from going where he wishes.

If I am able to determine the enemy's dispositions while, at the same time, I conceal my own, then I can concentrate my forces and his must be divided. And if I concentrate while he divides, I can use my entire strength to attack a fraction of his. Therefore, I will be numerically superior. Then, if I am able to use many to strike few at the selected point, those I deal with will fall into hopeless straits. The enemy must not know where I intend to give battle. For if he does not know where I intend to give battle, he must prepare in a great many places. And when he prepares in a great many places, those I have to fight will be few. For if he prepares to the front, his rear will be weak, and if to the rear, his front will be fragile. If he strengthens his left, his right will be vulnerable, and if his right, there will be few troops on his left. And when he sends troops everywhere, he will be weak everywhere. Numerical weakness comes from having to guard against possible attacks; numerical strength from forcing the enemy to make these preparations against us.

If one knows where and when a battle will be fought, his troops can march a thousand *li* and meet on the field. But if one knows neither the battleground nor the day of battle, the left will be unable to aid the right and the right will be unable to aid the left, and the van will be unable to support the rear and the rear, the van. How much more is this so when separated by several tens of *li* or, indeed, by even a few! Although I estimate the troops of Yüe as many, of what benefit is this superiority with respect to the outcome of war? Thus, I say that victory can be achieved. For even if the enemy is numerically stronger, I can prevent him from engaging.

Therefore, analyse the enemy's plans so that you will know his shortcomings as well as strong points. Agitate him in order to ascertain the pattern of his movement. Lure him out to reveal his dispositions and ascertain his position. Launch a probing attack in order to learn where his strength is abundant and where deficient. The ultimate in disposing one's troops is to conceal them without ascertainable shape. Then the most penetrating spies cannot pry nor can the wise lay plans against you. It is according to the situations that plans are laid for victory, but the multitude does not comprehend this. Although everyone can see the outward aspects, none understands how the victory is achieved. Therefore, when a victory is won, one's tactics are not repeated. One should always respond to circumstances in an infinite variety of ways.

Now, an army may be likened to water, for just as flowing water avoids the heights and hastens to the lowlands, so an army should avoid strength and strike weakness. And as water shapes its flow in accordance with the ground, so an army manages its victory in accordance with the situation of the enemy. And as water has no constant form, there are in warfare no constant conditions. Thus, one able to win the victory by modifying his tactics in accordance with the enemy situation may be said to be divine. Of the five elements [water, fire, metal, wood and earth], none is always predominant; of the four seasons, none lasts forever; of the days, some are long and some short, and the moon waxes and wanes. That is also the law of employing troops.

军争第七

　　孙子曰：凡用兵之法，将受命于君，合军聚众，交和而舍，莫难于军争。军争之难者，以迂为直，以患为利。故迂其途，而诱之以利，后人发，先人至，此知迂直之计者也。

　　故军争为利，军争为危。举军而争利，则不及；委军而争利，则辎重捐。是故卷甲而趋，日夜不处，倍道兼行，百里而争利，则擒三将军。劲者先，疲者后，其法十一而至；五十里而争利，则蹶上将军，其法半至；三十里而争利，则三分之二至。是故军无辎重则亡，无粮食则亡，无委积则亡。

　　故不知诸侯之谋者，不能豫交；不知山林、险阻、沮泽之形者，不能行军；不用乡导者，不能得地利。故兵以诈立，以利动，以分合为变者也。故其疾如风，其徐如林，侵掠如火，不动如山，难知如阴，动如雷震。掠乡分众，廓地分利，悬权而动。先知迂直之计者胜，此军争之法也。

　　《军政》曰："言不相闻，故为金鼓；视不相见，故为旌旗。"夫金鼓旌旗者，所以一人之耳目也；人既专一，则勇者不得独进，怯者不得独退，此用众之法也。故夜战多火鼓，昼战多旌旗，所以变人之耳目也。

故三军可夺气，将军可夺心。是故朝气锐，昼气惰，幕气归。故善用兵者，避其锐气，击其惰归，此治气者也。以治待乱，以静待哗，此治心者也。以近待远，以佚待劳，以饱待饥，此治力者也。无邀正正之旗，勿击堂堂之陈，此治变者也。

故用兵之法，高陵勿向，背丘勿逆，佯北勿从，锐卒勿攻，饵兵勿食，归师勿遏，围师必阙，穷寇勿迫，此用兵之法也。

CHAPTER 7

Manoeuvring

Normally, in war, the general receives his commands from the sovereign. During the process from assembling the troops and mobilising the people to blending the army into a harmonious entity and encamping it, nothing is more difficult than the art of manoeuvring for advantageous positions. What is difficult about it is to make the devious route the most direct and to turn disadvantage to advantage. Thus, march by an indirect route and divert the enemy by enticing him with a bait. So doing, you may set out after he does and arrive at the battlefield before him. One able to do this shows the knowledge of the artifice of diversion.

Therefore, both advantage and danger are inherent in manoeuvring for an advantageous position. One who sets the entire army in motion with impediments to pursue an advantageous position will not attain it. If he abandons the camp and all the impediments to contend for advantage the stores will be lost. Thus, if one orders his men to make forced marches without armour, stopping neither day nor night, covering double the usual distance at a stretch, and doing a hundred *li* to wrest an advantage, it is probable that the commanders will be captured. The stronger men will arrive first and the feeble ones will struggle along behind; so, if this method is used, only one-tenth of the army will reach its destination. In a forced march of fifty *li*, the commander of the van will probably fall, but half the army will arrive. In a forced march of thirty *li*, just two-thirds will arrive. It follows that an army which lacks heavy equipment, fodder, food and stores will be lost.

One who is not acquainted with the designs of his neighbours should not enter into alliances with them. Those who do not know the conditions of mountains and forests, hazardous defiles, marshes and swamps, cannot conduct the march of an army. Those who do not use local guides are unable to obtain the advantages of the ground. Now, war is based on deception. Move when it is advantageous and create changes in the situation by dispersal and concentration of forces. When campaigning, be swift as the wind; in leisurely marching, majestic as the forest; in raiding and plundering, be fierce as fire; in standing, firm as the mountains. When hiding, be as unfathomable as things behind the clouds; when moving, fall like a thunderbolt. When you plunder the countryside, divide your forces. When you conquer territory, defend strategic points. Weigh the situation before you move. He who knows the artifice of diversion will be victorious. Such is the art of manoeuvring.

The Book of Military Administration says: 'As the voice cannot be heard in battle, drums and gongs are used. As troops cannot see each other clearly in battle, flags and banners are used.' Now, gongs and drums, banners and flags are used to unify the action of the troops. When the troops can be thus united, the brave cannot advance alone, nor can the cowardly withdraw. This is the art of directing large masses of troops. In night fighting, use many torches and drums, in day fighting, many banners and flags, in order to guide the sight and hearing of our troops.

Now, an army may be robbed of its spirit and its commander deprived of his confidence. At the beginning of a campaign, the spirits of soldiers are keen; after a certain period time, they flag, and in the later stage thoughts turn towards home. And therefore, those skilled in war avoid the enemy when his spirit is keen and attack him when it is sluggish and his soldiers homesick. This is control of the moral factor. In good order, they await a disorderly enemy; in serenity, a clamorous one. This is control of the mental factor. Close to the field of battle, they await an enemy coming from afar; at rest, they await an exhausted enemy; with well-fed troops, they await hungry ones. This is control of the physical factor. They do not engage an enemy advancing with well-ordered banners nor one whose formations are in impressive array. This is control of the factor of changing circumstances.

Therefore, the art of employing troops is that when the enemy occupies high ground, do not confront him uphill, and when his back is resting on hills, do not make a frontal attack. When he pretends to flee, do not pursue. Do not attack troops whose spirits are keen. Do not swallow bait. Do not thwart an enemy who is returning homewards.

Leave a way of escape to a surrounded enemy, and do not press a desperate enemy too hard. Such is the art of employing troops.

九变第八

孙子曰：凡用兵之法，将受命于君，合军聚众，圮地无舍，衢地交合，绝地无留，围地则谋，死地则战。

涂有所不由，军有所不击，城有所不攻，地有所不争，君命有所不受。故将通于九变之利者，知用兵矣；将不通于九变之利者，虽知地形，不能得地之利矣；治兵不知九变之术，虽知五利，不能得人之用矣。

是故智者之虑，必杂于利害。杂于利，而务可信也；杂于害，而患可解也。

是故屈诸侯者以害，役诸侯者以业，趋诸侯者以利。

故用兵之法，无恃其不来，恃吾有以待也；无恃其不攻，恃吾有所不可攻也。

故将有五危：必死，可杀也；必生，可虏也；忿速，可侮也；廉洁，可辱也；爱民，可烦也。

凡此五者，将之过也，用兵之灾也。覆军杀将，必以五危，不可不察也。

CHAPTER 8

The Nine Variables

In general, the system of employing troops is that the commander receives his mandate from the sovereign to mobilise the people and assemble the army.

You should not encamp on grounds hard to approach. Unite with your allies on grounds intersected with highways. Do not linger on desolate ground. In enclosed ground, resort to stratagem. In death ground, fight a last-ditch battle.

There are some roads which must not be followed, some troops which must not be attacked, some cities which must not be assaulted, and some ground which should not be contested. There are also occasions when the commands of the sovereign need not be obeyed. Therefore, a general thoroughly versed in the advantages of the nine variable factors knows how to employ troops. One who does not understand their advantages will not be able to use the terrain to his advantage even though he is well acquainted with it. In the direction of military operations, one who does not understand the tactics suitable to the nine variable situations will be unable to use his troops effectively, even if he understands the 'five advantages' [referring to the five situations mentioned at the beginning of this paragraph].

And for this reason, a wise general in his deliberations must consider both favourable and unfavourable factors. By taking into account the favourable factors, he makes his plan feasible; by taking into account the unfavourable, he may avoid possible disasters.

He who wants to subdue dukes in neighbouring states does so by inflicting injury upon them. He who wants to control them does so by keeping them constantly occupied, and he who makes them rush about does so by offering them ostensible advantages.

It is a doctrine of war not to assume the enemy will not come but rather to rely on one's readiness to meet him, and not to presume that he will not attack but rather to make oneself invincible.

There are five qualities which are fatal in the character of a general: if reckless, he can be killed; if cowardly, captured; if quick-tempered, he can be provoked to rage and make a fool of himself; if he has too delicate a sense of honour, he can be easily insulted; if he is of a compassionate nature, you can harass him.

Now these five traits of character are serious faults in a general and in military operations are calamitous. The ruin of the army and the death of the general are inevitable results of these shortcomings. They must be deeply pondered.

行军第九

孙子曰：凡处军相敌：

绝山依谷，视生处高，战隆无登，此处山之军也。

绝水必远水，客绝水而来，勿迎之于水内，令半济而击之，利；欲战者，无附于水而迎客；视生处高，无迎水流，此处水上之军也。

绝斥泽，惟亟去无留；若交军于斥泽之中，必依水草，而背众树，此处斥泽之军也。

平陆处易，而右背高，前死后生，此处平陆之军也。

凡此四军之利，黄帝之所以胜四帝也。

凡军好高而恶下，贵阳而贱阴，养生而处实，军无百疾，是谓必胜。丘陵堤防，必处其阳，而右背之。此兵之利，地之助也。上雨，水沫至，欲涉者，待其定也。凡地有绝涧、天井、天牢、天罗、天陷、天隙，必亟去之，勿近也。吾远之，敌近之；吾迎之，敌背之。军行有险阻、潢井、葭苇、山林、翳荟者，必谨复索之，此伏奸之所处也。

敌近而静者，恃其险也；远而挑战者，欲人之进也；其所居易者，利也。众树动者，来也；众草多障者，疑也；鸟起者，伏也；兽骇者，覆也。

尘高而锐者，车来也；卑而广者，徒来也；散而条达者，樵采也；少而往来者，营军也。敌卑而益备者，进也；辞强而进驱者，退也；轻车先出居其侧者，陈也；无约而请和者，谋也；奔走而陈兵车者，期也；半进半退者，诱也。杖而立者，饥也；汲而先饮者，渴也；见利而不进者，劳也；鸟集者，虚也；夜呼者，恐也。

军扰者，将不重也；旌旗动者，乱也；吏怒者，倦也；粟马肉食，军无悬瓴，不返其舍者，穷寇也；谆谆翕翕，徐与人言者，失众也；数赏者，窘也；数罚者，困也；先暴而后畏其众者，不精之至也；来委谢者，欲休息也。兵怒而相迎，久而不合，又不相去，必谨察之。

兵非益多也，惟无武进，足以并力、料敌、取人而已。夫惟无虑而易敌者，必擒于人。

卒未亲附而罚之，则不服，不服则难用也。卒已亲附而罚不行，则不可用也。故令之以文，齐之以武，是谓必取。令素行以教其民，则民服；令不素行以教其民，则民不服。

令素行者，与众相得也。

CHAPTER 9

On the March

When an army takes up a position and confronts the enemy, it has to observe and judge the enemy situation. In doing so, it should pay attention to the following:

When crossing the mountains, be sure to stay close to valleys; when encamping, select high ground facing the sunny side; when high ground is occupied by the enemy, do not ascend to attack. So much for taking a position in mountains.

After crossing a river, you must move some distance away from it. When an advancing enemy crosses water, do not meet him in midstream. It is advantageous to allow half his force to cross and then strike. If you wish to give battle, do not confront your enemy near the water. Take a position on high ground facing the sun. Do not take a position at the lower reaches of the enemy. This relates to positions near a river.

Cross salt marshes speedily. Do not linger in them. If you encounter the enemy in the middle of a salt marsh, you must take a position close to grass and water with trees to your rear. This has to do with taking up a position in salt marshes.

On level ground, occupy a position which facilitates your action. With heights to your rear and right, the field of battle is to the front and the rear is safe. This is how to take up a position on level ground.

Generally, these are advantageous principles for encamping in the four situations named. By using them, the Yellow Emperor conquered his four neighbouring sovereigns. [Legend has it that the Yellow Emperor was the most ancient emperor in China; he reigned about five thousand years ago.]

In battle, all armies prefer high ground to low, and sunny places to shady. If an army occupies high ground, which is convenient for living, it will not suffer from countless diseases, and this will spell victory. When you come to hills, dikes, or embankments, you must take a position on the sunny side. These are all advantageous methods, gained from the help the ground affords. When rain falls in the upper reaches of a river and foaming water descends, those who wish to ford must wait until the waters subside. Where there are precipitous torrents such as 'heavenly wells', 'heavenly prisons', 'heavenly nets', 'heavenly traps' and 'heavenly cracks' – you must march speedily away from them. Do not approach them. Keep a distance from them and draw the enemy towards them. Face them and cause the enemy to put his back to them. When, on the flanks of the army, there are dangerous defiles or ponds covered with aquatic grasses where reeds and rushes grow, or forested mountains with dense tangled undergrowth, you must carefully search them out, for these are places where ambushes are laid and spies are hidden.

When the enemy is nearby but remains calm, he is depending on a favourable position. When he challenges battle from afar, he wishes to lure you to advance; when he is on easy ground, he must be in an advantageous position. When the trees are seen to move, it means the enemy is advancing. When many screens have been placed in the undergrowth, it is for the purpose of deception. Birds rising in flight are a sign that the enemy is lying in ambush; when the wild animals are startled and flee, the enemy is trying to take you unawares.

Dust spurting upwards in high straight columns indicates the approach of chariots. When it hangs low and is widespread, it betokens that infantry is approaching. When dust rises in scattered areas, the enemy is collecting and bringing in firewood; when there are numerous small patches which seem to come and go, he is encamping the army. When the enemy's envoys speak in humble terms, but the army continues preparations, that means it will advance. When their language is strong and the enemy pretentiously advances, these may be signs that the enemy will retreat. When light chariots first go out and take position on the flanks, the enemy is forming. When without a previous understanding the enemy asks for a truce, he must be plotting. When his troops march speedily and he parades his battle chariots, he is expecting to rendezvous with reinforcements. When half his force advances and half withdraws, he is attempting to decoy you. When his troops lean on their weapons, they are famished. When drawers of water drink before carrying it to camp, his troops are suffering from thirst. When the enemy sees an advantage but does not advance to seize it, he is fatigued. When birds gather above the enemies camp sites, they are unoccupied. When at night the enemy's camp is clamorous, it betokens nervousness.

When his troops are disorderly, the general has no prestige. When his flags and banners are shifted about constantly, he is in disarray. If the officers are short-tempered, they are exhausted. When the enemy feeds grain to the horses and kills its cattle for food, and when his troops neither hang up their cooking pots nor return to their shelters, the enemy is desperate. When the troops continually gather in small groups and whisper together, the general has lost the confidence of the army. Too frequent rewards indicate that the general is at the end of his resources; too frequent punishments that he is in acute distress. If the officers at first treat the men violently and later are fearful of them, it shows supreme lack of intelligence. When the enemy's troops march up angrily and, although facing you, neither join battle for a long time nor leave, the situation requires great vigilance and thorough investigation.

In war, numbers alone confer no advantage. It is sufficient if you do not advance relying on sheer military power. If you estimate the enemy situation correctly and then concentrate your strength to overcome the enemy, there is no more to it than this. He who lacks foresight and underestimates his enemy will surely be captured by him.

If troops are punished before their loyalty is secured, they will be disobedient. If not obedient, it is difficult to employ them. If troops have become attached to you, but discipline cannot be enforced, you cannot employ them. Thus, command them with civility but keep them under control by iron discipline, and it may be said that victory is certain. If orders are consistently carried out to instruct the troops, they will be obedient. If orders are not consistently carried out to instruct them, they will be disobedient.

If orders are consistently trustworthy and carried out, it shows that the relationship of a commander with his troops is satisfactory.

地形第十

孙子曰：地形有通者，有挂者，有支者，有隘者，有险者，有远者。我可以往，彼可以来，曰通；通形者，先居高阳，利粮道，以战则利。可以往，难以返，曰挂；挂形者，敌无备，出而胜之；敌若有备，出而不胜，难以返，不利。我出而不利，彼出而不利，曰支；支形者，敌虽利我，我无出也；引而去之，令敌半出而击之，利。隘形者，我先居之，必盈之以待敌；若敌先居之，盈而勿从，不盈而从之。险形者，我先居之，必居高阳以待敌；若敌先居之，引而去之，勿从也。远形者，势均，难以挑战，战而不利。

凡此六者，地之道也，将之至任，不可不察也。

故兵有走者，有弛者，有陷者，有崩者，有乱者，有北者。凡此六者，非天之灾，将之过也。

夫势均，以一击十，曰走；卒强吏弱，曰弛；吏强卒弱，曰陷；大吏怒而不服，遇敌怼而自战，将不知其能，曰崩；将弱不严，教道不明，吏卒无常，陈兵纵横，曰乱；将不能料敌，以少合众，以弱击强，兵无选锋，曰北。凡此六者，败之道也，将之至任，不可不察也。

夫地形者，兵之助也。料敌制胜，计险阨远近，上将之道也。知此而用战者必胜，不知此而用战者必败。故战道必胜，主曰无战，必战可也；战道不胜，主曰必战，无战可也。故进不求名，退不避罪，唯人是保，而利合于主，国之宝也。

视卒如婴儿，故可与之赴深溪；视卒如爱子，故可与之俱死。厚而不能使，爱而不能令，乱而不能治，譬若骄子不可用也。

知吾卒之可以击，而不知敌之不可击，胜之半也；知敌之可击，而不知吾卒之不可以击；胜之半也；知敌之可击，知吾卒之可以击，而不知地形之不可以战，胜之半也。故知兵者，动而不迷，举而不穷。故曰：知彼知己，胜乃不殆；知天知地，胜乃不穷。

CHAPTER 10

Terrain

Ground may be classified according to its nature as accessible, entangling, temporising, precipitous, distant, or having narrow passes. Ground which both we and the enemy can traverse with equal ease is called accessible. On such ground, he who first takes high sunny positions, and keeps his supply routes unimpeded, can fight advantageously. Ground easy to reach but difficult to get out of is called entangling. The nature of this ground is such that if the enemy is unprepared and you sally out, you may defeat him. If the enemy is prepared and you sally out, but do not win, and it is difficult for you to return, it is unprofitable. Ground equally disadvantageous for both the enemy and ourselves to enter is called temporising. The nature of this ground is such that although the enemy holds out a bait, I do not go forth but entice him by marching off. When I have drawn out half his force, I can strike him advantageously. If I first occupy narrow passes, I must block the passes and await the enemy. If the enemy first occupies such ground and blocks the defiles, I should not attack him; if he does not block them completely, I may do so. On precipitous ground, I must take a position on the sunny heights and await the enemy. If he first occupies such ground, I march off; I do not attack him. When at a distance from an enemy of equal strength, it is difficult to provoke battle and unprofitable to engage him.

These are the principles relating to six different types of ground. It is the highest responsibility of the general to inquire into them with the utmost care.

There are six conditions in which troops fail. These are: flight, insubordination, collapse in disorder, distress, disorganisation, and rout. None of these disasters can be attributed to natural causes, but to the fault of the general.

Other conditions being equal, if a force attacks one ten times its size, the result is flight. When soldiers are strong and officers weak, the army is insubordinate. When the officers are valiant and the soldiers ineffective, the result is collapse. When officers are angry and insubordinate, and on encountering the enemy rush into battle with no understanding of the feasibility of engaging and without awaiting orders from the commander, the army is in distress. When the general is morally weak and without authority, when his instructions and guidance are not enlightened, when there are no consistent rules to guide the officers and men, and when the formations are slovenly, the result is disorganisation. When a commander unable to estimate his enemy uses a small force to engage a large one, or weak troops to strike the strong, or when he fails to select shock troops for the van, the result is rout. When any of these six conditions prevails, the army is on the road to defeat. It is the highest responsibility of the general that he examine them carefully.

Conformation of the ground is of the greatest assistance in battle. Therefore, virtues of a superior general are to estimate the enemy situation, and to calculate distances and the degree of difficulty of the terrain so as to control victory. He who fights with full knowledge of these factors is certain to win; he who does not will surely be defeated. If the situation is one of victory, but the sovereign has issued orders not to engage, the general may decide to fight. If the situation is such that he cannot win, but the sovereign has issued orders to engage, he need not do so. And therefore, the general who in advancing does not seek personal fame, and in retreating is not concerned with disgrace, but whose only purpose is to protect the country and promote the best interests of his sovereign, is the precious jewel of the state.

A general regards his men as infants who will march with him into the deepest valleys. He treats them as his own beloved sons and they will stand by him unto death. If a general indulges his men but is unable to employ them, if he loves them but cannot enforce his commands, if the men are disorderly and he is unable to control them, they may be compared to spoiled children, and are useless.

If I know that my troops are capable of striking the enemy, but do not know that he is invulnerable to attack, my chance of victory is but half. If I know that the enemy is vulnerable to attack, but do not know that my troops are incapable of striking him, my chance of victory is but half. If I know that the enemy can be attacked and that my troops are capable of attacking him, but do not realize that the conformation of the ground makes fighting impracticable, my chance of victory is but half. Therefore, when those experienced in war move, they are never bewildered; when they act, their resources are limitless. And therefore, I say: Know the enemy, know yourself; your victory will never be endangered. Know the ground, know the weather; your victory will then be complete.

九地第十一

孙子曰：用兵之法，有散地，有轻地，有争地，有交地，有衢地，有重地，有圮地，有围地，有死地。

诸侯自战其地者，为散地。入人之地而不深者，为轻地。我得则利，彼得亦利者，为争地。我可以往，彼可以来者，为交地。诸侯之地三属，先至而得天下之众者，为衢地。入人之地深，背城邑多者，为重地。行山林、险阻、沮泽，凡难行之道者，为圮地。所由入者隘，所从归者迂，彼寡可以击吾之众者，为围地。疾战则存，不疾战则亡者，为死地。

是故散地则无战，轻地则无止，争地则无攻，交地则无绝，衢地则合交，重地则掠，圮地则行，围地则谋，死地则战。

所谓古之善用兵者，能使敌人前后不相及，从寡不相恃，贵贱不相救，上下不相收，卒离而不集，兵合而不齐。合于利而动，不合于利而止。敢问：敌众整而将来，待之若何？曰：先夺其所爱，则听矣。兵之情主速，乘人之不及，由不虞之道，攻其所不戒也。

凡为客之道：深入则专，主人不克；掠无饶野，三军足食；谨养而勿劳，并气积力；运兵计谋，为不可测。投之无所往，死且不北，死焉不得，士人尽力。兵士甚陷则不惧，无所往则固，深人则拘，不得已则斗。是故其兵不修而戒，不求而得，不约而亲，不令而信。禁祥去疑，至死无所之。吾士无杀财，非恶货也；无余命，非恶寿也。令发之日，士卒坐者涕霑襟，偃卧者涕交颐。投之无所往者，诸、刿之勇也。

故善用兵者，譬如率然；率然者，常山之蛇也。击其首则尾至，击其尾则首至，击其中则首尾俱至。敢问：兵可使如率然乎？曰：可。夫吴人与越人相恶也，当其同舟而济，遇风，其相救也，如左右手。是故方马埋轮，未足恃也；齐勇若一，政之道也；刚柔皆得，地之理也。故善用兵者，携手若使一人，不得已也。

将军之事，静以幽，正以治。能愚士卒之耳目，使之无知。易其事，革其谋，使人无识；易其居，迂其途，使人不得虑。帅与之期，如登高而去其梯；帅与之深入诸侯之地，而发其机，焚舟破釜，若驱群羊，驱而往，驱而来，莫知所之。聚三军之众，投之于险，此谓将军之事也。九地之变，屈伸之利，人情之理，不可不察。

凡为客之道，深则专，浅则散。去国越境而师者，绝地也；四达者，衢地也，人深者，重地也；人浅者，轻地也；背固前隘者，围地也；无所往者，死地也。是故散地，吾将一其志；轻地，吾将使之属；争地，吾将趋其后，交地，吾将谨其守；衢地，吾将固其结；重地，吾将继其食；圮地，吾将进其涂；围地，吾将塞其阙；死地，吾将示之以不活。故兵之情，围则御，不得已则斗，过则从。

　　是故不知诸侯之谋者，不能预交；不知山林、险阻、沮泽之形者，不能行军；不用乡导者，不能得地利。四五者，不知一，非霸、王之兵也。夫霸、王之兵，伐大国，则其众不得聚；威加于敌，则其交不得合。

　　是故不争天下之交，不养天下之权，信己之私，威加于敌，故其城可拔，其国可隳。施无法之赏，悬无政之令，犯三军之众，若使一人。犯之以事，勿告以言；犯之以利，勿告以害。投之亡地然后存，陷之死地然后生。夫众陷于害，然后能为胜败。故为兵之事，在于顺详敌之意，并敌一向，千里杀将，此谓巧能成事者也。

　　是故政举之日，夷关折符，无通其使；厉于廊庙之上，以诛其事。敌人开阖，必亟入之。先其所爱，微与之期。践墨随敌，以决战事。是故始如处女，敌人开户，后如脱兔，敌不及拒。

CHAPTER 11

The Nine Varieties of Ground

In respect to the employment of troops, ground may be classified as dispersive, frontier, key, open, focal, serious, difficult, encircled, and desperate.

When a feudal lord fights in his own territory, he is in dispersive ground. When he makes but a shallow penetration into enemy territory, he is in frontier ground. Ground equally advantageous to occupy is key ground. Ground equally accessible is open. When a state is enclosed by three other states, its territory is focal. He who first gets control of it will gain the support of the majority of neighbouring states. When the army has penetrated deep into hostile territory, leaving far behind many enemy cities and towns, it is in serious ground. When the army traverses mountains, forests, or precipitous country, or marches through defiles, marshlands or swamps, or any place where the going is hard, it is in difficult ground. Ground to which access is constricted, where the way out is tortuous, and where a small enemy force can strike a larger one, is called encircled. Ground in which the army survives only if it fights with the courage of desperation is called desperate. And therefore, do not fight in dispersive ground; do not stop in the frontier borderlands.

Do not attack an enemy who occupies key ground first; in open ground, do not allow your formations to become separated and your communications to be blocked. In focal ground, ally with neighbouring states; in serious ground, gather in plunder. In difficult ground, press on; in encircled ground, devise stratagems; in desperate ground, fight courageously.

In ancient times, those described as skilled in war made it impossible for the enemy to unite his front and his rear, for his divisions both large and small to cooperate, for his good troops to succour the poor, and for officers and men to support each other. When the enemy's forces were dispersed, they prevented him from assembling them; even when assembled, they threw him into disorder. They concentrated and moved when it was advantageous to do so; when not advantageous, they halted. Should one ask: 'How do I cope with a well-ordered enemy host about to attack me?' I reply: 'Seize something he cherishes and he will conform to your desires.' Speed is the essence of war. Take advantage of the enemy's unpreparedness, make your way by unexpected routes, and attack him where he has taken no precautions.

The general principles applicable to an invading force are that when you have penetrated deeply into hostile territory your army is united and the defender cannot overcome you. Plunder fertile country to supply your army with plentiful provisions. Pay heed to nourishing the troops; do not unnecessarily fatigue them. Unite them in spirit; conserve their strength. Make unfathomable plans for the movements of the army. Throw the troops into a position from which there is no escape, and even when faced with death they will not flee. For if prepared to die, what can they not achieve? Then officers and men together put forth their utmost efforts. In a desperate situation, they fear nothing; when there is no way out, they stand firm. Deep in a hostile land they are bound together, and there, where there is no alternative, they will engage the enemy in hand-to-hand combat. Thus, such troops need no encouragement to be vigilant. Without extorting their support, the general obtains it; without inviting their affection, he gains it; without demanding their discipline, he wins it. Prohibit superstitious doubts and do away with rumours; then nobody will flee even facing death. My officers have no surplus of wealth, but it is not because they disdain riches; they have no expectation of long life, but it is not because they dislike longevity. On the day the army is ordered to set out, the tears of those seated soak their garments – the tears of those reclining course down their cheeks. But throw them into a situation where there is no escape and they will display the immortal courage of Zhuan Zhu and Cao Kuei. [Zhuan Zhu and Cao Kuei both lived in the Spring and Autumn Period, and were said to be brave warriors undaunted in the face of death.]

Now, the troops of those adept in war are used like the 'simultaneously responding snake' of Mount Ch'ang. When struck on the head, its tail attacks; when struck on the tail, its head attacks; when struck in the centre, both head and tail attack. Should one ask: 'Can troops be made capable of such instantaneous coordination?' I reply. 'They can.' For, although the men of Wu and Yüeh hate one another, if together in a boat tossed by the wind they would cooperate as the right hand does with the left. Thus, in order to prevent soldiers from fleeing, it is not sufficient to rely upon hobbled horses or buried chariot wheels. To achieve a uniform level of valour relies on a good military administration. And it is by proper use of the ground that both strong and weak forces are used to the best advantage. Thus, a skilful general conducts his army just as if he were leading a single man, willy-nilly, by the hand.

It is the business of a general to be serene and inscrutable, impartial and self-controlled. He should be capable of keeping his officers and men in ignorance of his plans. He changes his methods and alters his plans so that people have no knowledge of what he aims at. He alters his camp sites and marches by devious routes, and thus makes it impossible for others to anticipate his purpose. The business of a general is to kick away the ladder behind soldiers when they have climbed up a height. He leads the army deep into hostile territory and there releases the trigger. He burns his boats and smashes his cooking pots; he drives his men now in one direction, then in another, like a shepherd driving a flock of sheep, and no one knows where he is going. To assemble the army and throw it into a desperate position is the business of the general. To take different measures suited to the nine varieties of ground, to take aggressive or defensive tactics in accordance with different situations, and to understand soldiers' psychological states under different circumstances, are matters that must be studied carefully by a general.

Generally, when invading hostile territory, the deeper one penetrates, the more cohesion it brings; penetrating only a short way causes dispersion. Therefore, in dispersive ground, I would unify the determination of the army. In frontier ground, I would keep my forces closely linked. In key ground, I would hasten into the enemy's rear. In open ground, I would pay strict attention to my defences. In focal ground, I would consolidate my alliances. In serious ground, I would ensure a continuous flow of provisions.

In difficult ground, I would march past the roads speedily. In encircled ground, I would block the points of access and egress. In desperate ground, I would make it evident that there is no chance of survival. For it is the nature of soldiers to resist when surrounded, to fight to the death when there is no alternative, and when desperate to follow commands implicitly.

One ignorant of the plans of neighbouring states cannot make alliances with them; if ignorant of the conditions of mountains, forests, dangerous defiles, swamps and marshes, he cannot conduct the march of an army; if he fails to make use of native guides, he cannot gain the advantages of the ground. A general ignorant of even one of these nine varieties of ground is unfit to command the armies of a hegemonic king. Now, when a hegemonic king attacks a powerful state, he makes it impossible for the enemy to concentrate his troops. He overawes the enemy and prevents his allies from joining him.

It follows that there is no need to contend against powerful combinations, nor is there any need to foster the power of other states. He relies for the attainment of his aims on his ability to overawe his opponents. And so he can take the enemy's cities and overthrow the enemy's state. Bestow rewards without respect to customary practice; publish orders without respect to precedent. Thus, you may employ the entire army as you would one man. Set the troops to their tasks without imparting your designs; use them to gain advantage without revealing the dangers involved. Throw them into a perilous situation and they will survive; put them in desperate ground and they will live. For when the army is placed in such a situation, it can snatch victory from defeat. Now, the crux of military operations lies in the pretence of following the designs of the enemy; and once there is a loophole that can be used, concentrate your forces against the enemy. Thus, even marching from a distance of a thousand *li*, you can kill his general. This is called the ability to achieve one's aim in an artful and ingenious manner.

Therefore, when the time comes to execute the plan to attack, you should close the passes, rescind the passports, have no further intercourse with the enemy's envoys, and exhort the temple council to execute the plans. When the enemy presents an opportunity, speedily take advantage of it. Seize the place which the enemy values without making an appointment for battle with him. In executing the plan, you should change according to the enemy situation in order to win victory. Therefore, at first you should pretend to be as shy as a maiden. When the enemy gives you an opening, be swift as a hare and he will be unable to withstand you.

火攻第十二

孙子曰：凡火攻有五：一曰火人，二曰火积，三曰火辎，四曰火库，五曰火队。行火必有因，烟火必素具。发火有时，起火有日。时者，天之燥也；日者，月在箕、壁、翼、轸也。凡此四宿者，风起之日也。

凡火攻，必因五火之变而应之。

火发于内，则早应之于外。火发兵静者，待而勿攻，极其火力，可从而从之，不可从而止。火可发于外，无待于内，以时发之。火发上风，无攻下风。昼风久，夜风止。凡军必知有五火之变，以数守之。

故以火佐攻者明，以水佐攻者强。水可以绝，不可以夺。

夫战胜攻取，而不修其功者凶，命曰费留。故曰：明主虑之，良将修之。非利不动，非得不用，非危不战。主不可以怒而兴师，将不可以愠而致战。合于利而动，不合于利而止。怒可以复喜，愠可以复悦，亡国不可以复存，死者不可以复生。故明君慎之，良将警之，此安国全军之道也。

CHAPTER 12

Attack By Fire

There are five ways of attacking with fire. The first is to burn soldiers; the second, to burn provisions; the third, to burn equipment; the fourth, to burn arsenals; and the fifth, to burn the lines of transportation. To use fire, some medium must be relied upon. Equipment for setting fires must always be at hand. There are suitable times and appropriate days on which to raise fires. 'Times' means when the weather is scorching hot; 'days' means when the moon is in Sagittarius, Alpharatz, *I*, or *Zhen* constellations, for these are days of rising winds.

Now, in fire attacks, one must respond to the changing situation. When fire breaks out in the enemy's camp, immediately coordinate your action from without. But if the enemy troops remain calm, bide your time and do not attack at once. When the fire reaches its height, follow up if you can. If you cannot do so, wait. If you can raise fires outside the enemy camp, it is not necessary to wait until they are started inside. Set fires at suitable times. When fires are raised upwind, do not attack from downwind. When the wind blows during the day, it will die down at night. Now, the army must know the five different fire attack situations and wait for appropriate times.

Those who use fire to assist their attacks can achieve good results; those who use inundations produce a powerful effect. Water can isolate an enemy, but cannot destroy his supplies or equipment as fire can.

Now, to win battles and take your objectives but to fail to consolidate these achievements is ominous and may be described as a waste of time. And therefore, it is said that enlightened rulers must deliberate upon the plans to go to battle, and good generals carefully execute them. If not in the interests of the state, do not act. If you cannot succeed, do not use troops. If you are not in danger, do not fight a war. A sovereign cannot launch a war because he is enraged, nor can a general fight a war because he is resentful. For while an angered man may again be happy, and a resentful man again be pleased, a state that has perished cannot be restored, nor can the dead be brought back to life. Therefore, the enlightened ruler is prudent and the good general is warned against rash action. Thus the state is kept secure and the army preserved.

用间第十三

孙子曰：凡兴师十万，出征千里，百姓之费，公家之奉，日费千金。内外骚动，怠于道路，不得操事者，七十万家。

相守数年，以争一日之胜，而爱爵禄百金，不知敌之情者，不仁之至也，非人之将也，非主之佐也，非胜之主也。故明君贤将，所以动而胜人，成功出于众者，先知也。先知者不可取于鬼神，不可象于事，不可验于度，必取于人，知敌之情者也。

故用间有五：有因间，有内间，有反间，有死间，有生间。五间俱起，莫知其道，是谓神纪，人君之宝也。因间者，因其乡人而用之。内间者，因其官人而用之。反间者，因其敌间而用之。死间者，为诳事于外，令吾间知之，而传于敌间也。生间者，反报也。

故三军之事，莫亲于间，赏莫厚于间，事莫密于间。非圣智不能用间，非仁义不能使间，非微妙不能得间之实。

微哉！微哉！无所不用间也。间事未发，而先闻者，间与所告者皆死。

凡军之所欲击，城之所欲攻，人之所欲杀，必先知其守将、左右、谒者、门者、舍人之姓名，令吾间必索知之。必索敌人之间来间我者，因而利之，导而舍之，故反间可得而用也。因是而知之，故乡间、内间可得而使也；因是而知之，故死间为诳事可使告敌；因是而知之，故生间可使如期。

　　五间之事，主必知之，知之必在于反间，故反间不可不厚也。

　　昔殷之兴也，伊挚在夏；周之兴也，吕牙在殷。故惟明君贤将能以上智为间者，必成大功。此兵之要，三军之所恃而动也。

CHAPTER 13

Use of Spies

Now, when an army of one hundred thousand is raised and dispatched on a distant campaign, the expenses borne by the people together with disbursements of the treasury will amount to a thousand pieces of gold daily. In addition, there will be continuous commotion both at home and abroad, people will be exhausted by the corvée of transport, and the farm work of seven hundred thousand households will be disrupted. [In ancient times, eight families comprised a community. When one family sent a man to the army, the remaining seven contributed to its support. Thus, when an army of one hundred thousand was raised, those unable to attend fully to their own ploughing and sowing amounted to seven hundred thousand households.]

Hostile armies confront each other for years in order to struggle for victory in a decisive battle; yet if one who begrudges rank, honours and a few hundred pieces of gold remains ignorant of his enemy's situation, he is completely unaware of the interest of the state and the people. Such a man is no general, no good assistant to his sovereign, and such a sovereign no master of victory. Now, the reason a brilliant sovereign and a wise general conquer the enemy whenever they move, and their achievements surpass those of ordinary men, is their foreknowledge of the enemy situation. This 'foreknowledge' cannot be elicited from spirits, nor from gods, nor by analogy with past events, nor by astrologic calculations. It must be obtained from men who know the enemy situation.

Now, there are five sorts of spies. These are native spies, internal spies, double spies, doomed spies, and surviving spies. When all these five types of spies are at work and their operations are clandestine, it is called the 'divine manipulation of threads' and is the treasure of a sovereign. Native spies are those from the enemy's country people whom we employ. Internal spies are enemy officials whom we employ. Double spies are enemy spies whom we employ. Doomed spies are those of our own spies who are deliberately given false information and told to report it to the enemy. Surviving spies are those who return from the enemy camp to report information.

Of all those in the army close to the commander, none is more intimate than the spies; of all rewards, none more liberal than those given to spies; of all matters, none is more confidential than those relating to spy operations. He who is not sage and wise, humane and just, cannot use spies. And he who is not delicate and subtle cannot get the truth out of them.

Delicate, indeed! Truly delicate! There is no place where espionage is not possible. If plans relating to spy operations are prematurely divulged, the agent and all those to whom he spoke of them should be put to death.

Generally, in the case of armies you wish to strike, cities you wish to attack, and people you wish to assassinate, it is necessary to find out the names of the garrison commander, the aides-de-camp, the ushers, gatekeepers and bodyguards. You must instruct your spies to ascertain these matters in minute detail. It is essential to seek out enemy spies who have come to conduct espionage against you and to bribe them to serve you. Give them instructions and care for them. Thus, double spies are recruited and used. It is by means of the double spies that native and internal spies can be recruited and employed. And it is by this means that the doomed spies, armed with false information, can be sent to convey it to the enemy. It is by this means also that surviving spies can come back and give information as scheduled.

The sovereign must have full knowledge of the activities of the five sorts of spies. And the key is the skill to use the double spies. Therefore, it is mandatory that they be treated with the utmost liberality.

In old times, the rise of the Shang Dynasty was due to Yi Zhi, who had served under the Xia likewise, and the rise of the Zhou Dynasty was due to Lu Ya, who had served under the Yin. And therefore, only the enlightened sovereign and the wise general who are able to use the most intelligent people as spies can achieve great results. Spy operations are essential in war; upon them the army relies to make its every move.